September 2013

DHS FINANCIAL MANAGEMENT

Additional Efforts Needed to Resolve Deficiencies in Internal Controls and Financial Management Systems

GAO Highlights

Highlights of GAO-13-561, a report to congressional requesters

DHS FINANCIAL MANAGEMENT

Additional Efforts Needed to Resolve Deficiencies in Internal Controls and Financial Management Systems

Why GAO Did This Study

In 2003, GAO designated DHS's management functions—including financial management—as high risk. Since obtaining a clean opinion on its financial statements and improving the effectiveness of internal controls are key aspects of DHS's strategy for addressing its high-risk financial management issues, GAO was asked to review DHS's efforts to strengthen its financial reporting, including how it plans to modernize its current financial systems. This report examines (1) DHS's progress toward obtaining clean opinions on its financial statements and internal control over financial reporting and (2) the extent to which DHS's approach for modernizing its current financial systems was consistent with OMB requirements and whether DHS followed certain IT best practices while implementing its approach. GAO interviewed key DHS officials, reviewed relevant DHS guidance and documents, and determined whether DHS followed OMB requirements and certain industry best practices.

What GAO Recommends

To help DHS deploy component-level integrated financial management systems, GAO is making four recommendations to DHS regarding the need to follow best practices related to its target state, transition plan, integrated master schedule, and lessons learned. DHS generally agreed with GAO's recommendations and described actions already taken to address them. GAO agrees that DHS has completed actions to address two recommendations, but further action is needed to address the others.

View GAO-13-561. For more information, contact Asif A. Khan at (202) 512-9869 or khana@gao.gov.

What GAO Found

The Department of Homeland Security (DHS) has made considerable progress toward obtaining a clean opinion on its financial statements but limited progress in obtaining a clean opinion on its internal control over financial reporting. DHS continues to rely on compensating controls and complex manual work-arounds rather than sound internal control over financial reporting and effective financial management systems. DHS is working to resolve the deficiencies that caused its auditors to issue a qualified opinion on its fiscal year 2012 financial statements and has a goal of achieving a clean opinion in fiscal year 2013. In addition, DHS has plans to resolve the remaining five material internal control weaknesses, with a goal of achieving a clean opinion on internal control over financial reporting for fiscal year 2016. However, DHS's auditors stated that they may have identified additional material weaknesses in fiscal year 2012 had they been able to perform sufficient work to enable them to express an opinion on the effectiveness of DHS's internal control over financial reporting. DHS will continue to face challenges in obtaining and sustaining a clean opinion on its financial statements and attaining a clean opinion on its internal control over financial reporting until serious internal control and financial management systems deficiencies are resolved.

DHS's decentralized approach for modernizing its components' financial systems is consistent with relevant Office of Management and Budget (OMB) requirements, such as implementing projects in smaller, simpler segments, but not all relevant information technology (IT) best practices have been fully implemented. DHS plans to modernize the financial systems of components with the most critical need first and integrate the financial systems with asset management and acquisition systems, resulting in component-level integrated financial management systems. DHS has implemented certain IT recommended best practices that reflect key areas of effective program management, such as conducting an analysis of alternatives, establishing a governance structure, developing baseline business process requirements, and developing a description of its current financial management environment. However, DHS has not yet fully incorporated other IT best practices that help improve the effectiveness of such implementation. Specifically, DHS has not developed (1) a description of how its components' financial management systems will operate in the future (detailed target state), (2) a description of how components will transition to a new financial management environment (department-level transition plan), (3) procedures for validating the completion of and updating the milestone dates for activities reflected in its integrated master schedule, and (4) procedures for addressing key elements of a lessons learned process. DHS plans to develop a target state and transition plan after its components award their financial system modernization contracts. DHS officials stated that validating and updating activities in the master schedule were covered by broader procedures. The officials also stated that they had sufficient procedures for identifying, documenting, and sharing lessons learned. Without a detailed target state, department-level transition plan, and specific procedures, DHS has an increased risk of, among other things, investing in and implementing systems that do not provide the desired capabilities and inefficiently using resources during its financial management system modernization efforts.

_____ United States Government Accountability Office

Contents

Letter		1
	Background	3
	DHS Has Made Considerable Progress toward a Clean Opinion on Financial Statements, but Needs to Achieve Sound Internal Control over Financial Reporting	5
	DHS's Financial Systems Modernization Approach Is Consistent with OMB Requirements, but Implementation Needs to Incorporate IT Best Practices	11
	Conclusions	19
	Recommendations for Executive Action	19
	Agency Comments and Our Evaluation	20
Appendix I	Scope and Methodology	26
Appendix II	Financial Management Actions and Outcomes for Addressing High-Risk Areas	28
Appendix III	Material Weaknesses at DHS for Fiscal Years 2005 through 2012	32
Appendix IV	Remaining Material Weaknesses at DHS	33
Appendix V	Comments from the Department of Homeland Security	35
Appendix VI	GAO Contact and Staff Acknowledgments	39
Tables		
	Table 1: Financial Audit Scope and Results for Fiscal Years 2005 through 2012 (dollars in billions)	7

Table 2: Internal Control over Financial Reporting Audit Results
and Number of Reported Material Weaknesses, Fiscal
Years 2005 through 2012   9
Table 3: High-Risk Financial Management Actions and Outcomes   28
Table 4: Auditor-Reported Material Weaknesses at DHS   32
Table 5: Fiscal Year 2012 Auditor-Reported Material Weaknesses
and Related Recommendations   33

Abbreviations

CFO	Chief Financial Officer
CFO Act	Chief Financial Officers Act of 1990
DHS	Department of Homeland Security
eMerge^2	Electronically Managing Enterprise Resources for Government Effectiveness and Efficiency
FEMA	Federal Emergency Management Agency
FFMIA	Federal Financial Management Improvement Act of 1996
ICE	Immigration and Customs Enforcement
IT	information technology
OCFO	Office of the Chief Financial Officer
OMB	Office of Management and Budget
PCIE	President's Council on Integrity and Efficiency
PP&E	property, plant, and equipment
SOP	standard operating procedures
TASC	Transformation and Systems Consolidation
USCG	U.S. Coast Guard

September 30, 2013

Congressional Requesters

Since the Department of Homeland Security's (DHS) inception in 2003, significant internal control and financial management system deficiencies have hampered its ability to manage operations and properly account for its assets, which it reported as totaling $87.2 billion as of September 30, 2012.[1] Further, we have previously reported that DHS's financial management internal control weaknesses impeded the department from providing reliable, timely, and useful financial data to support daily operational decision making. The internal control and financial management system deficiencies contributed to our decision to designate DHS's management functions, including financial management, as high risk.[2] As noted in our 2013 high-risk report, continued improvement is needed in order to mitigate the risks identified and to help ensure that management weaknesses do not hinder the department's ability to efficiently and effectively use its resources and accomplish its mission.

In 2004, legislation was enacted that required DHS to undergo annual financial audits and obtain assurances that it can generate timely, reliable, consistent, and accurate financial information for management

---

[1]The Federal Financial Management Improvement Act of 1996 defines "financial management systems" as the financial systems and the financial portions of mixed systems necessary to support financial management, including automated and manual processes, procedures, controls, data, hardware, software, and support personnel dedicated to the operation and maintenance of system functions. A "financial system" is an information system, comprising one or more applications, that is used for (1) collecting, processing, maintaining, transmitting, or reporting data about financial events; (2) supporting financial planning or budgeting activities; (3) accumulating and reporting costs information; or (4) supporting the preparation of financial statements. The term mixed systems refers to information systems that support both financial and nonfinancial functions of the federal government or its components.

[2]See GAO, *High-Risk Series: An Update*, GAO-13-283 (Washington, D.C.: February 2013), and *High-Risk Series: An Update*, GAO-03-119 (Washington, D.C.: January 2003). In 2013, GAO changed the name of this high-risk area from "Implementing and Transforming" to "Strengthening DHS Management Functions" to recognize DHS's progress in its implementation and transformation since its creation, as well as to focus on its remaining challenges in strengthening its management functions and integrating those functions across the department. The "Strengthening DHS Management Functions" high-risk area includes challenges in acquisition, information technology, human capital, and financial management.

analysis, decision making, and financial reporting.[3] DHS's past efforts to comply with this legislation have included addressing internal control weaknesses over processing and reporting of financial information and attempts to deploy integrated financial management systems. Nonetheless, the continued presence of significant internal control and financial management system deficiencies contributed to DHS's financial statements being unauditable from 2005 to 2010.[4]

Recognizing that obtaining an unmodified—or "clean"—opinion[5] on its financial statements and improving the effectiveness of internal controls are key aspects of DHS's strategy for addressing its high-risk financial management issues, you asked us to review the status of DHS's efforts to strengthen its financial reporting, including how it plans to modernize its current financial systems. For this report, we examined (1) DHS's progress toward obtaining clean opinions on its financial statements and its internal control over financial reporting,[6] and (2) the extent to which DHS's approach for modernizing its current financial systems was consistent with Office of Management and Budget (OMB) requirements and whether DHS's implementation of its approach followed certain information technology (IT) best practices.

DHS Management Functions High-Risk Area

In a September 2010 letter to DHS, we identified and DHS agreed to achieve 31 actions and outcomes that are critical to addressing the challenges within the department's management areas and integrating those functions across the department. The actions and outcomes are based on the issues we have identified and recommendations made through our wide-ranging work at DHS. Of the 31 actions and outcomes, 9 are related to financial management. See appendix II for additional information on the status of DHS's efforts to address the 9 high-risk financial management issues.

---

[3]Department of Homeland Security Financial Accountability Act, Pub. L. No. 108-330, 118 Stat. 1275 (Oct. 16, 2004).

[4]DHS's financial statements consist of the consolidated balance sheet; statements of net cost, changes in net position, budgetary resources, and custodial activity; and related notes.

[5]According to the American Institute of Certified Public Accountants' *Forming an Opinion and Reporting on Financial Statements* (AU-C Section 700), effective for audits of financial statements for periods ending on or after December 15, 2012, an unmodified opinion states that the financial statements are presented fairly, in all material respects, in accordance with the applicable accounting principles. For periods ending before December 15, 2012, an unmodified opinion was known as an unqualified opinion. For the purposes of this report, we use the term clean opinion to refer to either an unmodified opinion or an unqualified opinion.

[6]According to GAO's and the President's Council on Integrity and Efficiency's (PCIE) *GAO/PCIE Financial Audit Manual*, the objectives of internal control over financial reporting are to provide reasonable assurance that (1) transactions are properly recorded, processed, and summarized to permit the preparation of the financial statements in conformity with U.S. generally accepted accounting principles, and assets are safeguarded against loss from unauthorized acquisition, use, or disposition, and (2) transactions are executed in accordance with laws governing the use of budget authority and with other laws and regulations that could have a direct and material effect on the financial statements.

To determine the progress DHS has made toward obtaining clean opinions on both its financial statements and its internal control over financial reporting,[7] we interviewed DHS officials, reviewed fiscal year 2012 and prior years' audit results, and analyzed relevant documents. We also reviewed the reported internal control deficiencies and DHS's corrective actions to address them.[8] To determine whether DHS's approach for modernizing its current financial systems was consistent with OMB requirements, we interviewed DHS officials and reviewed applicable policy, procedure, and planning documents. Finally, to determine whether DHS's implementation of its financial systems modernization approach followed selected best practices, we identified the relevant IT best practices and reviewed available planning documents. Appendix I provides a more detailed discussion of our scope and methodology.

We conducted this performance audit from May 2012 to September 2013 in accordance with generally accepted government auditing standards. Those standards require that we plan and perform the audit to obtain sufficient, appropriate evidence to provide a reasonable basis for our findings and conclusions based on our audit objectives. We believe that the evidence obtained provides a reasonable basis for our findings and conclusions based on our audit objectives.

Background

In March 2003, DHS was created by merging 22 disparate agencies and organizations, many of which had known financial management weaknesses and vulnerabilities. Only 5 of the agencies that transferred to DHS had been subject to financial statement audits—U.S. Customs Service, Transportation Security Administration, Immigration and Naturalization Service, Federal Emergency Management Agency (FEMA), and Federal Law Enforcement Training Center.

---

[7]According to the American Institute of Certified Public Accountants' *An Examination of an Entity's Internal Control Over Financial Reporting That Is Integrated With an Audit of Its Financial Statements* (AT Section 501), a clean or unqualified opinion, in relation to an examination of an entity's internal control over financial reporting, states that in the auditors' opinion the entity maintained effective internal control over financial reporting. In other words, auditors determined the entity achieved the objectives of internal control over financial reporting.

[8]A deficiency in internal control exists when the design or operation of a control does not allow management or employees, in the normal course of performing their assigned functions, to prevent, or detect and correct, misstatements on a timely basis.

In October 2004, seeking to improve DHS's financial management, Congress passed the DHS Financial Accountability Act, which amended the Chief Financial Officers Act of 1990 (CFO Act)[9] and designated DHS as a CFO Act agency. CFO Act agencies are required to, among other things, annually prepare department-wide audited financial statements,[10] and to comply with the Federal Financial Management Improvement Act of 1996 (FFMIA).[11] The DHS Financial Accountability Act also requires DHS to obtain an audit opinion on its internal control over financial reporting after fiscal year 2005, making DHS the only CFO Act agency explicitly required by law to do so. In addition, the DHS Financial Accountability Act required GAO to review and report on a study of the potential costs and benefits of requiring agencies subject to the CFO Act to obtain audit opinions on their internal control over financial reporting. In September 2006, we reported that auditor opinions on internal control over financial reporting are an important component of monitoring the effectiveness of an entity's risk management and accountability system.[12]

In December 2012, Congress passed the DHS Audit Requirement Target Act of 2012.[13] That act requires DHS to take the necessary steps to ensure that its fiscal year 2013 financial statements are ready in a timely manner in order to obtain a clean opinion. If DHS does not obtain a clean opinion on the financial statements, the act requires DHS to include in its annual financial report its plans to (1) obtain a clean opinion on its full set of financial statements, including its plans and resources needed to meet the act's deadlines; (2) eliminate significant deficiencies and material

---

[9]Pub. L. No. 101-576, 104 Stat. 2838 (Nov. 15, 1990).

[10]Before being designated a CFO Act agency, DHS was required under the Accountability of Tax Dollars Act of 2002, Pub. L. No. 107-289, 116 Stat. 2049 (Nov. 7, 2002), to obtain annual financial statement audits.

[11]Pub. L. No. 104-208, div. A, title VIII, 110 Stat. 3009, 3009-389 (Sept. 30, 1996).

[12]GAO, *Internal Control: Analysis of Joint Study on Estimating the Costs and Benefits of Rendering Opinions on Internal Control over Financial Reporting in the Federal Environment*, GAO-06-255R (Washington, D.C.: Sept. 6, 2006).

[13]Pub. L. No. 112-217, 126 Stat. 1591 (Dec. 20, 2012).

weaknesses in internal control over financial reporting,[14] including deadlines for the elimination of such deficiencies and weaknesses; and (3) modernize the financial management systems of the department, including timelines, goals, alternatives, and costs related to modernizing its financial management systems and associated financial controls.

For nearly a decade, DHS tried to modernize its financial management systems by attempting to implement a department-wide integrated financial management system. DHS's prior efforts included the Electronically Managing Enterprise Resources for Government Effectiveness and Efficiency (eMerge[2]) project and the Transformation and Systems Consolidation (TASC) program. DHS spent about $52 million on the eMerge[2] project, which lasted 2 years—from January 2004 through December 2005—when DHS acknowledged that the pilot project had not been successful. DHS spent about $4.2 million on the TASC program, which lasted 4 years—from June 2007 through June 2011—when DHS recognized that its requirements had changed and canceled the program.

DHS Has Made Considerable Progress toward a Clean Opinion on Financial Statements, but Needs to Achieve Sound Internal Control over Financial Reporting

DHS has made considerable progress toward obtaining a clean opinion on its financial statements. However, DHS's auditors indicated that DHS continues to rely on compensating controls and complex manual work-arounds because of a lack of effective controls. DHS has a goal of obtaining a clean opinion on its fiscal year 2013 financial statements. Without sound internal control over financial reporting, DHS's ability to efficiently manage its operations and resources on a daily basis and routinely provide useful, reliable, and timely financial information for decision making—as well as to obtain and sustain a clean opinion on its financial statements—is seriously hindered.

DHS auditors have reported a reduction in the number of material weaknesses in DHS's internal control over financial reporting. Some of the reductions were the result of DHS's auditors consolidating the

---

[14]A significant deficiency is a deficiency, or combination of deficiencies, in internal control important enough to merit attention by those charged with governance. A material weakness is a significant deficiency, or a combination of significant deficiencies, in internal control such that there is a reasonable possibility that a material misstatement of the entity's financial statements will not be prevented, or detected and corrected, on a timely basis.

reported material weaknesses. DHS developed a multiyear plan for resolving the remaining material weaknesses and set a goal for obtaining a clean opinion on the effectiveness of its internal control over financial reporting for fiscal year 2016.[15]

Financial Statements: Reduction in Audit Qualifications Resulted in Qualified Audit Opinion for Fiscal Year 2012

High-Risk Financial Management Actions and Outcomes

Two high-risk financial management actions and outcomes contain requirements concerning DHS's financial statements. One calls for DHS to expand the scope of the audit to obtain an opinion on all of the basic financial statements. A second outcome calls for DHS to obtain and then sustain a clean opinion on its financial statements for at least 2 consecutive years. (See app. II, actions and outcomes nos. 4 and 5.)

DHS has made considerable progress toward its goal, established in fiscal year 2011, of obtaining a clean opinion on its fiscal year 2013 financial statements. This progress includes

- reducing the number of audit qualifications from 11 in 2005 to 1 in 2010;[16]
- receiving a qualified audit opinion on two of its five fiscal year 2011 financial statements—the consolidated balance sheet and statement of custodial activity;
- expanding the financial audit in fiscal year 2012 to all financial statements; and
- obtaining a qualified opinion on the fiscal year 2012 financial statements.[17]

DHS was able to achieve this progress based in part on management's commitment to improving its financial management process. For example, DHS requires each component's Chief Financial Officer (CFO) to certify on a monthly basis that the financial data submitted to DHS's Office of the Chief Financial Officer (OCFO) is complete and accurate and supported by transactions recorded in the financial system. However, the auditors' report indicates that DHS continues to rely on compensating controls and complex manual work-arounds rather than sound internal control over

---

[15]Department of Homeland Security, *FY 2013-FY 2016 DHS Multi-Year Plan Internal Control over Financial Reporting,* Living Document Version 1 (Washington, D.C.: Apr. 30, 2013).

[16]An audit qualification is a matter identified by auditors that contributes to their inability to render a clean opinion on the financial statements.

[17]A qualified opinion, in relation to the financial statements, states that certain reported balances are unauditable, the financial statements contain a material departure from generally accepted accounting principles, or both.

financial reporting and effective financial management systems and related processes.[18]

Table 1 provides an overview of DHS's financial audit results since the enactment of the DHS Financial Accountability Act in 2004.

Table 1: Financial Audit Scope and Results for Fiscal Years 2005 through 2012 (dollars in billions)

	Fiscal year							
	2005	**2006**	**2007**	**2008**	**2009**	**2010**	**2011**	**2012**
Audit scope	Limited: balance sheet	Limited: balance sheet and statement of custodial activity	Limited: balance sheet and statement of custodial activity	Limited: balance sheet and statement of custodial activity	Limited: balance sheet and statement of custodial activity	Limited: balance sheet and statement of custodial activity	Limited: balance sheet and statement of custodial activity	Full scope: all financial statements
Total assets[a]	$114.5 unaudited	$79.2 unaudited	$78.8 unaudited	$87.9 unaudited	$84.8 unaudited	$90.1 unaudited	$86.9 audited	$87.2 audited
Audit results/ opinion	Disclaimer[b]	Disclaimer	Disclaimer	Disclaimer	Disclaimer	Disclaimer	Qualified	Qualified
Number of audit qualifications	11	10	6	4	3	1	1	1
Number of DHS components contributing to audit qualifications	6	6	3	3	2	1	1	1

Source: DHS's annual financial audit reports.

[a]Total assets are the resources owned or managed by DHS that represent future economic benefits.

[b]A disclaimer of opinion states that the auditor does not express an opinion on whether the financial statements are free of significant errors and comply with applicable accounting principles because of—among other things—the lack of supporting documents or restrictions imposed by management that significantly limit the scope of the audit.

DHS received a disclaimer of opinion on the financial statements from fiscal years 2005 to 2010 before obtaining a qualified opinion on its consolidated balance sheet and statement of custodial activity for fiscal year 2011. For fiscal year 2012, DHS was unable to obtain a clean opinion on its entire set of financial statements because of the U.S. Coast Guard's (USCG) inability to complete certain reconciliations and provide

---

[18]Department of Homeland Security, Office of Inspector General, *Independent Auditors' Report on DHS' FY 2012 Financial Statements and Internal Control over Financial Reporting*, OIG-13-20 (Washington, D.C.: Nov. 14, 2012).

GAO-13-561 DHS Financial Management

evidence supporting certain components of general property, plant, and equipment (PP&E) and heritage and stewardship assets. As a result, the auditors deemed $8.3 billion, or approximately 40 percent of DHS's PP&E, as unauditable. According to DHS officials, USCG is working to develop and implement policies, procedures, and internal controls to improve its reporting of PP&E balances and heritage and stewardship assets in fiscal year 2013.

Internal Control over Financial Reporting: Auditors Did Not Issue an Opinion in 2012 Because of Material Weaknesses

DHS has made limited progress toward obtaining a clean opinion on the effectiveness of its internal control over financial reporting. For the past 4 years, the severity of DHS's internal control deficiencies has prevented DHS's auditors from performing sufficient work to enable them to express an audit opinion on the effectiveness of DHS's internal control over financial reporting. Although the number of auditor-reported material weaknesses in DHS's internal control over financial reporting has decreased since fiscal year 2005, as noted in table 2, the largest reduction—for fiscal year 2007—was due to a consolidation of weaknesses into fewer, broader categories for reporting purposes.[19] In accordance with auditing standards, DHS will have to eliminate all material weaknesses at the department level in order to receive a clean opinion on the effectiveness of its internal control over financial reporting.[20]

Table 2 provides an overview of the results of the audits of DHS's internal control over financial reporting since the enactment of the DHS Financial

[19]For fiscal year 2007, auditors consolidated certain material weaknesses by combining (1) intragovernmental balances into the financial reporting material weakness; (2) PP&E with the operating materials and supplies material weakness and reporting the combination as capital assets and supplies; and (3) actuarial liabilities with the legal and other liabilities and reported the combination as actuarial and other liabilities. The auditors noted that DHS had made progress during fiscal year 2007 in remediating the deficiency related to intragovernmental balances. The USCG was the only DHS component that contributed to the fiscal year 2006 material weaknesses in operating materials and supplies and actuarial liabilities, but the auditors did not report that USCG had made progress during fiscal year 2007 in remediating the deficiencies within operating materials and supplies and actuarial liabilities.

[20]American Institute of Certified Public Accountants, *Statements on Standards for Attestation Engagements: An Examination of an Entity's Internal Control Over Financial Reporting That Is Integrated With an Audit of Its Financial Statements*, AT Section 501 (New York).

Accountability Act in 2004. Appendix III provides a summary of the reported material weaknesses at DHS for fiscal years 2005 through 2012.

Table 2: Internal Control over Financial Reporting Audit Results and Number of Reported Material Weaknesses, Fiscal Years 2005 through 2012

	Fiscal year							
	2005	2006	2007	2008	2009	2010	2011	2012
Audit results	Not applicable	Adverse[a]	Adverse	Adverse	Disclaimer[b]	Disclaimer	Disclaimer	Disclaimer
Number of material weaknesses	10	10	7[c]	6	6	6	5	5
Number of DHS components contributing to material weaknesses	6	8	8	8	8	7	7	8
Number of deficiencies contributing to material weaknesses	30	28	24	22	24	18	15	17

Source: DHS's annual financial audit reports.

Note: The DHS Office of Inspector General examined DHS's internal control over financial reporting during fiscal years 2006, 2007, and 2008. Since fiscal year 2009, an independent public accounting firm has performed the examination of DHS's internal control over financial reporting as part of the audit of DHS's financial statements.

[a]An adverse opinion, in relation to an entity's internal control over financial reporting, states that in the auditors' opinion the entity has ineffective internal control over financial reporting because one or more material weaknesses exist.

[b]A disclaimer of opinion, in relation to an entity's internal control over financial reporting, states that the auditors do not express an opinion on the effectiveness of an entity's internal control over financial reporting because of, for example, management not providing supporting evidence, which restricts the auditors' scope of work needed to assess the effectiveness of internal control over financial reporting.

[c]For fiscal year 2007, DHS's auditors reduced the number of reported material weaknesses from 10 to 7 by consolidating the weaknesses into fewer, broader categories for reporting purposes.

From fiscal years 2005 through 2011, the auditors reported a reduction in the number of material weaknesses in internal control over financial reporting from 10 to 5 and a decrease in the number of control deficiencies contributing to the material weaknesses from 30 to 15.

For fiscal year 2012, the most recently completed audit, DHS's auditors reported material weaknesses in the following areas: (1) financial reporting, (2) IT controls and financial system functionality, (3) PP&E, (4) environmental and other liabilities, and (5) budgetary accounting. According to DHS's auditors, the existence of these material weaknesses limits DHS's ability to process, store, and report financial data in a manner that ensures accuracy, confidentiality, integrity, and availability of data without substantial manual intervention. This, in turn, increases the risk that human error may cause material misstatements in the financial statements. DHS's auditors stated that additional material weaknesses may have been identified and reported for fiscal year 2012 had the auditors been able to perform sufficient work to enable them to express an opinion on the effectiveness of DHS's internal control over financial reporting.[21] DHS will continue to experience difficulties in establishing sound internal control over financial reporting until DHS addresses serious financial management system deficiencies, such as system functionality issues. See appendix IV for additional information regarding the remaining material weaknesses at DHS and the auditors' recommendations.

High-Risk Financial Management Actions and Outcomes

Three high-risk financial management actions and outcomes contain requirements concerning DHS's internal control over financial reporting. One requires DHS top management's continuous commitment to correcting identified weaknesses, monitoring the status of corrective actions, and establishing and maintaining effective financial management internal controls. Another action and outcome calls for implementing a corrective action plan with specific milestones, while a third calls for obtaining an opinion on internal control over financial reporting. (See app. II, actions and outcomes nos. 1, 2, and 4.)

In April 2013, DHS issued a multiyear plan for resolving the remaining five material weaknesses. This plan included focusing its remediation efforts on specific material weaknesses each year. For example, DHS planned to mitigate the PP&E material weakness in fiscal year 2013. DHS's remediation activities included developing and implementing processes, policies, and procedures; improving supervision and monitoring of transactions; and maintaining supporting documentation. In commenting on our draft report, DHS stated that it had updated its multiyear plan and now plans to resolve the budgetary accounting material weakness in fiscal year 2013 and the PP&E material weakness in fiscal year 2014. Because of the severity of the remaining material weaknesses—and considering its timeline for addressing financial management system deficiencies through its modernization efforts—DHS has set a goal of fiscal year 2016 for obtaining a clean opinion on the effectiveness of its internal control over financial reporting.

---

[21]The auditors stated that the scope of their work was not sufficient to express an opinion on the effectiveness of DHS's internal control over financial reporting because of (1) USCG's inability to complete certain reconciliations and provide evidence supporting certain components of general PP&E and heritage and stewardship assets and (2) DHS's qualified assurance regarding the effectiveness of its internal control over financial reporting because of the existence of material weaknesses.

DHS's Financial Systems Modernization Approach Is Consistent with OMB Requirements, but Implementation Needs to Incorporate IT Best Practices

DHS is pursuing a decentralized approach for modernizing its components' financial systems. The approach includes both an incremental development aspect and top management oversight, both of which are consistent with relevant OMB requirements for financial system modernization.[22] Although components are in the early planning stages of implementing the approach, DHS has implemented some best practices, such as requiring components to conduct an analysis of alternatives and establishing a governance structure.[23] However, DHS has not yet fully incorporated other IT best practices that are intended to help improve the effectiveness of such implementations.[24] Specifically, DHS has not developed (1) a description of its future financial management system environment (target state),[25] (2) a description of how components will transition to the target state (transition plan),[26] (3) procedures for validating the completion of and updating the milestones dates for

---

[22]Office of Management and Budget, *Improving Financial Systems Through Shared Services*, Memorandum No. M-13-08 (Washington, D.C.: Mar. 25, 2013); *Federal Information Technology Shared Services Strategy* (Washington, D.C.: May 2, 2012); and *Immediate Review of Financial Systems IT Projects*, Memorandum No. M-10-26 (Washington, D.C.: June 28, 2010).

[23]Institute of Electrical and Electronics Engineers, *IEEE Guide for Information Technology – System Definition – Concept of Operations (ConOps) Document*, Standard 1362™-1998 (Dec. 5, 2007), and Office of Management and Budget, *Preparation, Submission and Execution of the Budget*, Circular No. A-11, Section 51.19 (Washington, D.C.: Aug. 3, 2012), and Memorandum No. M-10-26.

[24]GAO, *GAO Schedule Assessment Guide: Best Practices for Project Schedules*, exposure draft, GAO-12-120G (Washington, D.C.: May 2012); GAO, *GAO Cost Estimating and Assessment Guide: Best Practices for Developing and Managing Capital Program Costs*, GAO-09-3SP (Washington, D.C.: March 2009); GAO, *Information Technology Investment Management: A Framework for Assessing and Improving Process Maturity*, GAO-04-394G (Washington, D.C.: March 2004); GAO, *NASA: Better Mechanisms Needed for Sharing Lessons Learned*, GAO-02-195 (Washington, D.C.: Jan. 30, 2002); Office of Management and Budget, *The Common Approach to Federal Enterprise Architecture* (Washington, D.C.: May 2012); Carnegie Mellon Software Engineering Institute, *Capability Maturity Model® Integration for Acquisition (CMMI-ACQ), Improving Processes for Acquiring Better Products and Services*, ver. 1.3 (November 2010); and IEEE Standard 1362™-1998.

[25]The target state or architecture is the desired future state for an entity within the context of a strategic direction.

[26]A transition plan is a high-level, step-by-step guide for moving from the current state to the target state.

activities reflected in its integrated master schedule,[27] and (4) procedures for addressing key elements of a lessons learned process.

DHS's Financial Systems Modernization Approach Is Consistent with OMB Requirements, and Components Are in the Early Planning Stage

DHS has established a decentralized approach for modernizing its components' financial systems that is consistent with OMB financial system modernization requirements.[28] In line with current OMB requirements, DHS's decentralized approach involves incremental development and top management oversight. DHS components plan to provide financial system capabilities to end users in small increments within 6 to 12 months and complete individual financial system modernization projects in 18 to 24 months.[29] DHS's decentralized approach also calls for modernizing the financial systems of components with the most critical need first. Based on analysis performed during one of DHS's prior system modernization efforts—the TASC program—DHS prioritized Immigration and Customs Enforcement (ICE), USCG, and FEMA.

Additionally, DHS requires each component seeking to modernize its financial system to evaluate migrating to a federal shared service provider, in line with OMB requirements, as part of its analysis of alternatives.[30] Because of DHS's size, DHS officials expressed concern over the capacity and availability of the federal shared service providers.[31] In addition to components modernizing their financial systems that are used for financial reporting, DHS's end goal is to deploy component-level integrated financial management systems, which include those financial

---

[27]An integrated master schedule is a document that incorporates the planned work, the resources necessary to accomplish that work, and the associated budget.

[28]OMB Memorandum No. M-10-26 calls for agencies to implement IT projects with simpler segments and clear deliverables, focus on the most critical business needs first, and place a priority on senior agency managers monitoring projects on an ongoing basis.

[29]Financial system capabilities include general ledger management, cost management, payment management, receivable management, funds management, and reporting.

[30]Office of Management and Budget, *Federal Information Technology Shared Services Strategy.*

[31]According to OMB Memorandum No. M-13-08, OMB, along with the Department of the Treasury, plans to conduct an assessment of the capabilities and gaps of existing federal shared service providers. The memorandum does not provide a time frame for performing the assessment.

systems and the financial portion of other mixed systems.[32] Specifically, the components' integrated financial management systems will consist of not only a financial system, but also an asset management system and acquisition system.[33]

As part of its decentralized approach, DHS has established a financial management system modernization governance structure that includes top management oversight. Specifically, the governance structure includes the Financial Systems Modernization Executive Steering Committee and DHS's Under Secretary for Management. The Financial Systems Modernization Executive Steering Committee is chaired by the DHS CFO and comprises management chiefs such as the Chief Information Officer, Chief Procurement Officer, and component CFOs. The committee is charged with providing oversight and guidance to ensure that component modernization projects align with department and component strategic goals and objectives and with recommending component financial system selections to the Under Secretary for Management. Components seeking to modernize their financial systems must obtain approval from the Under Secretary for Management prior to expending any funds.

Both ICE and USCG are in the early planning stages of implementing DHS's decentralized approach and have evaluated various alternatives, such as improving their current financial systems, replacing or upgrading their systems, and acquiring the services of a federal shared service provider. ICE is conducting further alternative evaluations that are scheduled for completion in September 2013, while USCG has completed its evaluation and is seeking approval from the Under Secretary for Management to migrate to a federal shared service provider. DHS's goal is to reach a decision on the modernization of ICE's and USCG's financial systems by the end of fiscal year 2013.

Additionally, ICE and USCG are DHS internal shared service providers that provide financial management services, which include financial

High-Risk Financial Management Actions and Outcomes

Three high-risk financial management actions and outcomes relate to DHS financial system modernization efforts. Specifically, one action and outcome calls for DHS to commit sufficient resources with the necessary financial management expertise to execute the corrective actions needed to implement its current approach for financial system modernization. An additional action and outcome involves DHS establishing contractor oversight mechanisms to monitor the contractor(s) selected to implement new or upgrade existing component financial systems. A third action and outcome requires DHS to successfully implement new or upgrade existing components' financial systems, as needed, throughout the department, including those at Immigration and Customs Enforcement, U.S. Coast Guard, and FEMA. (See app. II, actions and outcomes nos. 3, 8, and 9.)

---

[32]See footnote 1.

[33]In general, financial management systems can also include, for example, payroll, travel, grants, insurance, and loans systems.

services, to eight other DHS components.[34] According to OCFO officials, DHS's modernization approach entails each component determining the specific solution for its financial system needs. Under this approach, each of ICE's and USCG's eight customers could pursue a different alternative for modernizing its financial systems if the customer develops a valid justification.

FEMA had postponed its modernization efforts while it addressed time-sensitive, critical stability issues with its legacy financial system. According to DHS officials, FEMA considered moving to a shared service provider as part of its modernization efforts, but the migration was anticipated to take up to 18 months, and FEMA determined that its legacy system could not sustain operations for that length of time given its deficiencies. To continue sustaining operations of its legacy financial system, FEMA stated that it improved its existing infrastructure to stabilize the system for another 3 to 5 years. FEMA completed this effort in May 2013 and anticipates restarting its modernization efforts and conducting an analysis of alternatives in fiscal year 2014.

DHS's Early Implementation of Its Approach Is Not Fully Consistent with IT Best Practices

DHS has implemented certain IT recommended best practices to help manage and guide it and its components as they implement the decentralized approach, but it has not yet developed certain documentation or fully incorporated other IT best practices. In addition to requiring components to conduct an analysis of alternatives and establishing the governance structure previously described, DHS has also developed a (1) description of its current financial management environment and (2) financial management systems baseline business process requirements and common data standards, such as a standard accounting classification structure.[35]

---

[34]ICE provides financial management services to six customer components—the U.S. Citizenship and Immigration Services, National Protection and Programs Directorate, Science and Technology Directorate, Office of Health Affairs, United States Visitor and Immigrant Status Indicator Technology, and DHS Headquarters. USCG provides financial management shared services to two customer components—the Transportation Security Administration and Domestic Nuclear Detection Office. According to DHS's auditors, certain ICE and USCG control and systems deficiencies affect their customers' financial management.

[35]GAO-04-394G and IEEE Standard 1362™-1998.

Although these IT best practices reflect key areas of effective program management and provide valuable information to help guide components' financial management system modernization projects, DHS has not developed documentation that provides

- a description of how its components' financial management systems will operate in the future (target state) and
- a description of how components will transition from the current financial management environment to the target state (transition plan).

While DHS has drafted standard operating procedures (SOP) for other IT best practices, the draft SOPs do not fully incorporate

- procedures for validating the completion of activities listed and revising milestone dates in its department-level integrated master schedule, which DHS recognizes is a critical tool for effectively monitoring its components' projects and for which it has developed draft procedures, and
- procedures for addressing key elements of a lessons learned process, such as specific procedures for identifying lessons learned.

Target state: IT best practices recommend having a well documented target state so that an organization can make effective decisions about IT investments.[36] In designing and implementing its modernization efforts, DHS has not developed a detailed description of its target state to help it and its components make effective investment decisions about financial management system investments, including financial systems. For example, DHS has not developed important details, such as department-level operational needs and characteristics, including the systems' availability, data flow, expandability, and interoperability. A detailed target state describes the technical aspect of the modernized systems in both technical and nontechnical terms to increase stakeholder understanding of how all of the various components' financial management systems would interact with each other and how information would flow among those systems.

DHS's Chief Architect described DHS's current target state as a "conceptual target state" lacking technical details, and DHS indicated that it plans to use the acquisition process to further define and document its

---

[36]GAO-04-394G and IEEE Standard 1362™-1998.

target state. DHS officials stated that a target state cannot be completed because components have not yet awarded their contracts for modernizing their financial systems. However, the target state should be developed before contracts are awarded so that DHS can make effective investment decisions. For example, without a detailed target state DHS's contracting decisions may be hampered by the lack of a thorough understanding of the technical aspect of components' financial management systems. This situation increases DHS's risk of investing in and implementing systems that do not provide the desired capabilities and do not interact efficiently.

Transition plan: Along with a target state, IT best practices recommend developing a related plan for transitioning from the current system environment to the future system environment.[37] A transition plan documents the tasks, milestones, and time frame for implementing new systems and establishes the optimal sequencing of activities. However, DHS has not developed a department-level transition plan in accordance with IT best practices for transitioning from its current financial management environment to the future financial management environment. According to DHS officials, similar to their plan for completing the target state, the transition plan will be developed after components award their contracts for modernizing their financial systems. Since DHS is attempting to modernize its components' systems concurrently, a department-level transition plan may help DHS effectively manage and implement its modernization approach. Without a detailed department-level transition plan, DHS may not be able to effectively and efficiently allocate and use resources for completing activities related to its financial management system modernization efforts.

Integrated master schedule: The use of an integrated master schedule is a well-established practice in program and project management and is a necessary tool for coordination of independently managed projects that have dependencies on one another.[38] The OCFO has developed a department-level integrated master schedule for monitoring the progress

---

[37]GAO-04-394G.

[38]GAO-12-120G and GAO-09-3SP.

of components' financial system modernization projects.[39] Although we did not assess DHS's integrated master schedule against all best practices for project schedules, we noted that the timelines did not reflect the current status and the schedule was not updated as required. Best practices indicate that for effective management of projects, the integrated master schedule should be updated regularly, depending on the project's duration, complexity, and risk,[40] which would provide DHS management information on the status of components' financial system modernization projects.

OCFO officials told us—and a related draft DHS SOP dated April 2013 requires—that OCFO staff update the master schedule on a regular basis (e.g., weekly). However, we noted that numerous activities in the February 2013 master schedule had completion dates occurring in 2012, yet the schedule indicated that the activities had not begun. OCFO officials told us that some activities had not occurred while others had been completed. They had not updated the schedule because components had not provided, for example, revised milestone dates and written confirmation of completed activities. Although the draft SOP required components to update the department-level master schedule on a regular basis, it did not have specific procedures for revising milestone dates and providing written confirmation of completed activities to the OCFO. OCFO officials stated that they did not include in the SOP specific procedures for components to revise milestone dates and to provide confirmation of completed activities because they thought those requirements were already covered by other broader procedures. Unless OCFO's staff receives and maintains up-to-date information on each component's project within the master schedule, DHS's efforts to measure each project's progress and identify potential problems may be impaired.

Lessons learned: Use of lessons learned is a principal component of an organizational culture committed to continuous improvement as well as effective project management. IT best practices call for identifying both positive and negative lessons learned within and outside the

---

[39]DHS OCFO requires each component with a financial system modernization project to develop a project schedule that will be used to update DHS OCFO's department-level integrated master schedule.

[40]GAO-12-120G.

organization.[41] We found that DHS identified and considered some lessons learned from its earlier system modernization efforts. For example, DHS learned that system modernization efforts should include a broad governance program that considers all relevant stakeholders. DHS's financial management system modernization governance structure includes a Financial Management Systems Working Group led by the OCFO and comprising cross-component financial systems subject matter experts. The group's responsibilities include fostering collaboration and information sharing across the department.

Although DHS considered some lessons learned from past financial management system modernization efforts, it did not have an organized process for consistently and systematically identifying, documenting, and sharing relevant lessons learned. IT industry best practices recommend having policies, processes, and procedures that address key elements of a lessons learned process, including identifying, documenting, and sharing lessons.

DHS was in the process of developing an SOP to formally document its financial management system modernization lessons learned process. The draft SOP, dated March 2013, contained an overview of DHS's lessons learned process; assigned responsibilities, including identifying and documenting lessons learned, to various entities, such as the Financial Systems Modernization Executive Steering Committee and Financial Management Systems Working Group; and discussed the use of databases to document and share lessons learned.

While the draft SOP contained general information that is useful for formally implementing the lessons learned process, it lacked specific procedures for addressing each of the key elements of the lessons learned process. For example, with the exception of internal lessons learned reviews, the draft SOP did not identify specific internal and external sources and suggested procedures for obtaining lessons learned from those sources. DHS officials told us that they have gathered lessons learned from both internal and external sources through market research and surveys that focus on financial system modernization, but the draft SOP did not include procedures for using these sources.

---

[41]Carnegie Mellon Software Engineering Institute, CMMI-ACQ Version 1.3; GAO-04-394G; and GAO-02-195.

Additionally, DHS officials stated that they also identified lessons learned from senior DHS personnel with prior system modernization experience at other federal agencies. However, the draft SOP did not contain procedures for documenting and sharing DHS personnel's prior relevant experiences. OCFO officials told us that the draft SOP sufficiently described how lessons learned were to be identified, documented, and shared. Without specific procedures that ensure thorough and consistent identification and consideration of lessons learned, the department risks overlooking beneficial information related to its prior modernization efforts, as well as those of other agencies, which may be leveraged to increase the success of current and future financial management system modernization projects.

Conclusions

Through continued reliance on compensating controls and complex manual work-arounds, DHS may achieve a clean opinion on its fiscal year 2013 financial statements while it works to address its remaining material weaknesses and system deficiencies. DHS will continue to face challenges to establishing effective internal control over financial reporting because of the lack of effective financial systems and related processes. Fully incorporating IT best practices related to its target state, transition plan, integrated master schedule, and lessons learned would help DHS improve its ability to achieve its end goal of deploying component-level integrated financial management systems, which are critical to establishing strong financial management. Strong financial management includes sound internal controls that safeguard assets and ensure proper accountability, as well as financial management systems that provide reliable, timely, and useful information to support day-to-day decision making and oversight.

Recommendations for Executive Action

To help DHS and its components improve their ability to achieve DHS's end goal of deploying component-level integrated financial management systems, we recommend that the Acting Secretary of Homeland Security direct the Under Secretary for Management to take the following four actions in accordance with industry best practices:

- develop a detailed target state that describes both in technical and nontechnical terms how its various components' financial management systems will interact with each other and how information will flow among those systems;

- develop and implement a department-level transition plan for moving from DHS's current financial management environment to the future financial management environment;
- update the SOP related to the department-level integrated master schedule to include specific procedures for components to revise milestone dates and provide the OCFO written confirmation of completed activities to maintain accurate and timely information within the master schedule; and
- include in the SOP for financial management system modernization specific procedures for consistently and systematically performing key elements of a lessons learned process, including identifying lessons learned using both internal and external sources and documenting and sharing relevant lessons learned.

Agency Comments and Our Evaluation

We provided a draft of this report to DHS for review and comment. In its written comments, which are reprinted in appendix V, DHS generally agreed with our recommendations and requested that they be considered resolved and closed based on actions it had already taken to address them. We agree that DHS has completed actions to address two recommendations, but further action is needed to address the other two. DHS also expressed concern regarding our presentation of certain information in our report. In addition, DHS provided technical comments, which we incorporated into the report as appropriate.

In regard to our four recommendations, DHS had the following comments.

- DHS concurred with our first recommendation to develop a detailed target state that describes—in both technical and nontechnical terms—its future components' financial management system environment. DHS agreed that a target state is essential, but asserted that it had already developed a target state in various documents for its modernization efforts and requested that our recommendation be considered resolved and closed. We agree that DHS has published various documents that define aspects of a target state for its financial management environment, including financial management systems baseline business process requirements and common data standards to help ensure consistent reporting of financial information. However, DHS has not developed other important details, such as department-level operational needs and characteristics, including the systems' availability, data flow, expandability, and interoperability. Such information would, among other things, help to increase stakeholders' understanding of both the department's and components' desired systems' capabilities. DHS's Chief Architect described DHS's current target state as a "conceptual target state" lacking technical details, and DHS indicated that it plans to use the acquisition process to further define and document its target state. As we state in our report, IT best practices recommend having a completed, detailed target state to help in the investment decision (acquisition) process. Thus, we consider our recommendation open until DHS takes appropriate action to address it. We modified our report to include (1) an example of the detailed information DHS needs to develop and (2) the Chief Architect's description of DHS's target state.

- DHS also concurred with our second recommendation, which called for it to develop and implement a transition plan for moving from DHS's current financial management environment to its future financial management environment. In its letter, DHS indicated that its financial system modernization approach document contains its transition strategy and requested that our second recommendation be considered resolved and closed. We determined that DHS's transition strategy does not contain needed elements of a transition plan referred to in our report, such as milestones and time frames for implementing new systems as well as the optimal sequencing of activities. DHS also stated that its transition strategy calls for each component to develop and implement an individual transition plan. We have modified the report to make it clear that DHS had not developed a department-level transition plan in accordance with IT best practices and that our recommendation was directed at the need for a department-level plan. DHS further stated that each component's transition plan may be constrained by available funding and external factors. Since DHS plans to modernize its components' systems concurrently and the lack of funding may constrain its efforts, we reiterate our statement in our report that a department-level transition plan would help DHS effectively and efficiently allocate and use available resources. Given that DHS has not developed a department-level transition plan, we consider our second recommendation open until DHS takes appropriate action to address it.

- Finally, DHS concurred with our third and fourth recommendations related to draft SOPs. After we provided our draft report to DHS for comment, DHS revised and finalized its SOPs on August 8, 2013, to include specific procedures to address our recommendations. Specifically, for the third recommendation related to the integrated master schedule, DHS established procedures for revising milestone dates and providing written confirmation of completed activities to the OCFO. For our fourth recommendation on DHS's financial

GAO-13-561 DHS Financial Management

management system modernization lessons learned process, DHS established procedures for performing key elements of a lessons learned process, including identifying lessons learned using both internal and external sources and documenting and sharing relevant lessons learned. We determined that DHS's actions to finalize its draft SOPs address the intent of these recommendations and should assist the OCFO in effectively measuring the progress of each component's modernization project, identifying potential problems related to a project, and reducing the risk of DHS overlooking beneficial lessons learned, which may increase the success of current and future financial management system modernization projects.

In commenting on our draft report, DHS expressed concern regarding our presentation of certain information in our report. Specifically, DHS expressed concern that we credit its fiscal year 2012 audit success to "herculean efforts, including complex workarounds that compensated for a lack of effective controls." DHS stated that the extraordinary efforts that made the full-scope audit possible were primarily focused on USCG, where complex work-arounds were required to compensate for a lack of automated systems controls. However, DHS's auditors reported that the agency continues to rely on compensating controls and complex manual work-arounds because of a lack of effective controls at other significant components, not just at USCG. The auditors also reported that the material weaknesses identified limit DHS's ability to process, store, and report financial data in a manner that ensures accuracy, confidentiality, integrity, and availability of data without substantial manual intervention. Although we believe the statement accurately describes the efforts DHS expended during the fiscal year 2012 audit, we have modified our report to provide a description of DHS's actions to compensate for the lack of effective controls, as indicated in the auditors' report.

DHS also commented on the statement in our draft report that its auditors may have identified additional material weaknesses had they been able to perform sufficient work to enable them to express an opinion on DHS's internal control over financial reporting. DHS agreed that the information was factual, but indicated that its auditors had used standard language for a disclaimer of opinion and did not have specific significant concerns regarding any unidentified material weaknesses. Additionally, DHS stated that the auditors made the statement in conjunction with their fiscal year 2012 scope limitation that dealt only with components of general PP&E and heritage and stewardship assets at USCG. We do not agree that the information as presented is misleading or that the auditors' concerns were limited to USCG. The auditors clearly communicated the possibility of identifying additional material weaknesses had they been able to perform sufficient work. Additionally, the auditors reported that the disclaimer of opinion on DHS's internal controls was based on specific deficiencies at USCG and the department's qualified assurance resulting from the existence of material weaknesses related to deficiencies at eight components, including USCG. To provide more context, we added a footnote to our report that presents the reasons the auditors cited for their fiscal year 2012 disclaimer of opinion on the effectiveness of DHS's internal control over financial reporting.

In an additional comment, DHS indicated that we should provide information on the significant progress DHS made in remediating deficiencies related to the material weaknesses its auditors combined for fiscal year 2007. We do acknowledge within our report that DHS has made progress in remediating material weaknesses since 2005. However, we do not agree with DHS's statement that the auditor reduced the number of material weaknesses in 2007, in part, because of significant progress achieved by DHS. The auditors specifically state that the reduction in material weaknesses is due to a consolidation for reporting purposes. To address DHS's comment, we provided more context by adding a footnote to our report that (1) lists the material weaknesses that the auditors combined and (2) presents information regarding the progress DHS made in fiscal year 2007 within the related areas as reported by its auditors.

DHS also stated that we did not fully recognize the significant steps it has taken to establish and implement its financial systems modernization approach. As indicated in our report, DHS has developed a decentralized approach to modernizing its financial systems, and components are in the early planning stage of implementing its approach. Our report acknowledges that DHS has implemented certain IT recommended best practices, such as a governance structure, to help manage and guide it and its components as they implement the decentralized approach. However, as we state in our report, DHS has not yet fully developed a detailed target state and department-level transition plan. As a result, DHS is at increased risk of investing in and implementing systems that do not provide the desired capabilities and inefficiently using resources during its financial management system modernization efforts.

As agreed with your offices, unless you publicly announce the contents of this report earlier, we plan no further distribution until 30 days from the report date. At that time, we will send copies to the Acting Secretary of

Homeland Security, the DHS Under Secretary for Management, and the DHS Chief Financial Officer. In addition, the report will be available at no charge on the GAO website at http://www.gao.gov.

If you or your staff have any questions about this report, please contact me at (202) 512-9869 or khana@gao.gov. Contact points for our Offices of Congressional Relations and Public Affairs may be found on the last page of this report. GAO staff members who made key contributions to this report are listed in appendix VI.

Asif A. Khan
Director
Financial Management and Assurance

List of Requesters

The Honorable Thomas R. Carper
Chairman
The Honorable Tom Coburn, M.D.
Ranking Member
Committee on Homeland Security and Governmental Affairs
United States Senate

The Honorable Claire McCaskill
Chairman
Subcommittee on Financial and Contracting Oversight
Committee on Homeland Security and Governmental Affairs
United States Senate

The Honorable Jeff Duncan
Chairman
Subcommittee on Oversight and Management Efficiency
Committee on Homeland Security
House of Representatives

Appendix I: Scope and Methodology

To determine the Department of Homeland Security's (DHS) progress toward obtaining unqualified (clean) opinions on both its financial statements and internal control over financial reporting, we interviewed DHS financial management officials and reviewed and analyzed DHS's fiscal year 2012 and prior annual financial reports as well as other relevant documents, such as DHS's *Internal Control Playbook, FY2013-FY2016 Multi-Year Plan on Internal Control over Financial Reporting*, and *Integrated Strategy for High Risk Management*. We performed our interviews and analytical reviews to identify reported audit qualifications and control deficiencies and determine the corrective actions DHS took to resolve the audit qualifications and remediate control deficiencies. We performed audit procedures to determine the extent to which we could use the work of DHS's auditors. Specifically, we assessed the financial auditors' independence, objectivity, and qualifications and reviewed audit planning and results documents.

To determine the extent to which DHS's approach for modernizing its current financial systems was consistent with Office of Management and Budget (OMB) requirements,[1] we interviewed DHS financial management officials and reviewed applicable policy, procedure, and planning documents, such as *DHS Approach to Financial Systems Modernization, Financial Systems Modernization Playbook*, and components' financial system modernization proposals. To determine whether DHS's implementation of its financial system modernization approach followed

---

[1]Office of Management and Budget, *Improving Financial Systems Through Shared Services*, Memorandum No. M-13-08 (Washington, D.C.: Mar. 25, 2013); *Federal Information Technology Shared Services Strategy* (Washington, D.C.: May 2, 2012); and *Immediate Review of Financial Systems IT Projects*, Memorandum No. M-10-26 (Washington, D.C.: June 28, 2010).

certain information technology (IT) best practices,[2] we limited our identification of best practices to those relevant to early planning of an IT project, such as the Institute of Electrical and Electronics Engineers standards, because DHS is just beginning to implement its approach and components' system modernization projects were in their early planning stage. Through our review of IT guidance and prior GAO reports, we identified best practices that recommend analyzing alternatives, establishing top management oversight, developing business requirements, developing a description of the current environment and target state and a transition plan, maintaining an integrated master schedule, and developing an IT lessons learned process. We assessed DHS's financial system modernization planning documents and draft standard operating procedures for its integrated master schedule and lessons learned process against the best practices we identified. Our scope did not include assessing the completeness of the integrated master schedule or determining the extent to which the schedule was developed in accordance with all IT best practices, nor did it include assessing the extent to which DHS incorporated actual lessons learned from its prior modernization efforts into its current financial systems modernization approach.

We conducted this performance audit from May 2012 to September 2013 in accordance with generally accepted government auditing standards. Those standards require that we plan and perform the audit to obtain sufficient, appropriate evidence to provide a reasonable basis for our findings and conclusions based on our audit objectives. We believe that the evidence obtained provides a reasonable basis for our findings and conclusions based on our audit objectives.

---

[2]GAO, *GAO Schedule Assessment Guide: Best Practices for Project Schedules*, exposure draft, GAO-12-120G (Washington, D.C.: May 2012); GAO, *GAO Cost Estimating and Assessment Guide: Best Practices for Developing and Managing Capital Program Costs*, GAO-09-3SP (Washington, D.C.: March 2009); GAO, *Information Technology Investment Management: A Framework for Assessing and Improving Process Maturity*, GAO-04-394G (Washington, D.C.: March 2004); GAO, *NASA: Better Mechanisms Needed for Sharing Lessons Learned*, GAO-02-195 (Washington, D.C.: Jan. 30, 2002); Office of Management and Budget, *The Common Approach to Federal Enterprise Architecture* (Washington, D.C.: May 2012); Office of Management and Budget, *Preparation, Submission and Execution of the Budget*, Circular No. A-11, Section 51.19 (Washington, D.C.: Aug. 3, 2012); Carnegie Mellon Software Engineering Institute, *Capability Maturity Model® Integration for Acquisition (CMMI-ACQ), Improving Processes for Acquiring Better Products and Services*, ver. 1.3 (November 2010); and Institute of Electrical and Electronics Engineers, *IEEE Guide for Information Technology – System Definition – Concept of Operations (ConOps) Document*, Standard 1362™-1998 (Dec. 5, 2007).

Appendix II: Financial Management Actions and Outcomes for Addressing High-Risk Areas

Based on our review of the Department of Homeland Security's (DHS) efforts, we determined that DHS has made progress related to improving its financial management and fully addressing two of the nine high-risk financial management actions and outcomes—obtaining top management commitment and developing corrective action plans. However, a significant amount of work remains to be completed on the remaining seven financial management actions and outcomes. We found that DHS still needs to obtain and sustain an unmodified (clean) opinion on its financial statements,[1] address weaknesses in internal controls and systems to obtain an opinion on the effectiveness of internal control over financial reporting, ensure that its financial systems substantially comply with the Federal Financial Management Improvement Act of 1996 (FFMIA), and deploy modern financial systems at certain components.[2] Table 3 shows our assessment of DHS's progress toward addressing the nine high-risk financial management actions and outcomes as of June 2013 using DHS-defined assessment categories and criteria.

Table 3: High-Risk Financial Management Actions and Outcomes

GAO financial management actions and outcomes[a]	Status of high-risk financial management actions and outcomes (as of June 2013)
Outcome No. 1: *Top Management Commitment* - Maintain top management commitment to correcting identified weaknesses, monitoring the status of corrective actions, and establishing and maintaining effective financial management internal controls.	DHS's management has fully addressed this outcome by demonstrating its sustained attention and focus on improving financial management. For example, DHS's Secretary publically committed to obtaining an audit opinion on its financial statements, DHS's Chief Financial Officer (CFO) meets monthly with components regarding their corrective action plans, and component CFOs are held accountable for meeting certain targets and milestones through their performance ratings. DHS has also established a governance structure—including the Financial Systems Modernization Executive Steering Committee—that will provide recommendations to DHS's Under Secretary for Management as well as oversight and guidance for financial system modernization efforts.[b] In addition, component heads are required to provide annual audit readiness assurance statements.

[1] Both an unmodified opinion and an unqualified opinion state that the financial statements are presented fairly in accordance with the applicable accounting principles. The term unmodified opinion applies to audits of financial statements for periods ending on or after December 15, 2012. Unqualified opinion applies to audits of financial statements for periods ending before December 15, 2012. Since our report covers periods before and after December 15, 2012, we use the term clean opinion to refer to both unmodified and unqualified audit opinions.

[2] DHS has determined that components with a critical business need to modernize their financial management systems include Immigration and Customs Enforcement and the U.S. Coast Guard, and their customer components, as well as the Federal Emergency Management Agency.

GAO financial management actions and outcomes[a]	Status of high-risk financial management actions and outcomes (as of June 2013)
Outcome No. 2: *Corrective Action Plan -* Develop and demonstrate measurable progress in implementing a corrective action plan with specific milestones and accountable officials to address the weaknesses in systems, internal control and business process weaknesses, and variations that impede DHS's ability to integrate and transform its financial management.	DHS has fully addressed this outcome by implementing a corrective action planning process and demonstrating measurable progress in correcting reported audit qualifications and internal control deficiencies. DHS annually prepares its *Internal Control Playbook*, which includes corrective action plans with specific milestones and accountable officials to address previously identified weaknesses over financial reporting and internal control operating efficiencies. From fiscal year 2005 to fiscal year 2012, DHS reduced the number of audit qualifications from 11 to 1, material weaknesses in internal control over financial reporting from 10 to 5,[c] and component conditions contributing to material weaknesses from 30 to 17 through its implementation of corrective action plans.
Outcome No. 3: *Commit Sufficient Resources* - Commit sufficient resources with the necessary financial management expertise to execute the corrective actions needed to implement its current approach for financial system modernization and complete a full-scope audit of the entire department's basic financial statements while addressing the weaknesses in financial management controls.	DHS has partially addressed this outcome by, for example, temporarily realigning resources to achieve audit goals such as sending DHS CFO staff members and contractors to support the U.S. Coast Guard's (USCG) efforts to eliminate an audit qualification related to its Fund Balance with Treasury. Additionally, DHS is supplementing funding for the Federal Emergency Management Agency's (FEMA) financial systems modernization efforts. However, to fully address this outcome, DHS needs to identify and commit the resources needed for modernizing its components' financial systems and remediating the remaining material weaknesses and significant deficiencies in its internal control over financial reporting. DHS has yet to develop a resource plan(s) that ensures sufficient resources with the necessary financial management expertise will be committed when needed.
Outcome No. 4: *Opinion on All of the Basic Financial Statements* - Expand the scope of the DHS financial statement audit to include an opinion on all of the basic financial statements as identified by Office of Management and Budget Circular A-136, including the required supplementary stewardship information and obtaining an opinion on internal control over financial reporting in accordance with the DHS Financial Accountability Act.	DHS has partially addressed this outcome by expanding its fiscal year 2012 financial statement audit to a full-scope audit and receiving a qualified audit opinion from its auditor on the financial statements. DHS has established a goal of obtaining a clean opinion on its fiscal year 2013 financial statements. According to DHS, it is moving closer to obtaining an opinion on its internal control over financial reporting by providing a qualified assurance statement on the effectiveness of those controls for fiscal year 2012. In April 2013, DHS published a multiyear plan for resolving the remaining five material weaknesses. As part of the multiyear plan, DHS has set a goal of fiscal year 2016 for obtaining a clean opinion on the effectiveness of its internal control over financial reporting.
Outcome No. 5: *Clean Opinions for 2 Years -* Sustain clean opinions for at least 2 consecutive years on the department-wide financial statements, while demonstrating measurable progress toward achieving effective internal controls by reducing material weaknesses and significant deficiencies. This should include establishing and standardizing effective business processes and financial management controls department-wide to avoid using ad hoc procedures, expending significant resources, and making billions of dollars in adjustments to derive clean opinions.	DHS has partially addressed this outcome by, among other things, demonstrating measurable progress in reducing its material weaknesses, obtaining a qualified opinion on its fiscal year 2012 financial statements, and working toward standardizing its business processes by issuing its financial management policy manual and systems standards. To fully address this outcome, DHS needs to obtain and sustain a clean opinion for 2 consecutive years on its financial statements without expending significant resources and making significant adjustments to obtain the clean opinions. Sustaining clean opinions on financial statements for at least 2 consecutive years is a criterion for DHS's removal from our high-risk list, as it has been for other federal agencies.

GAO financial management actions and outcomes[a]	Status of high-risk financial management actions and outcomes (as of June 2013)
Outcome No. 6: *Compliance with FFMIA* - Adhere to financial system requirements in accordance with FFMIA, and have independent auditors report annually on compliance with the act.	DHS has initiated efforts to address this outcome by, in part, having one of six components' financial systems substantially compliant with FFMIA requirements. To fully address this outcome, DHS needs to have the financial systems of all six components assessed (as a whole) by independent auditors as substantially compliant with FFMIA requirements. DHS's independent auditors have continually reported DHS's financial management systems as noncompliant with FFMIA since fiscal year 2005—the first year DHS's auditors were required to report on DHS's financial management systems' compliance with FFMIA.
Outcome No. 7: *Embrace Best Practices* - Embrace best practices, including those developed by the Institute of Electrical and Electronics Engineers and the Software Engineering Institute, when developing and documenting the department's current financial systems modernization strategy; and plan to foster the development of financial systems that meet expected performance and functionality targets.	DHS has initiated efforts to address this outcome by requiring components to comply with the DHS system engineering life cycle guide as they proceed with their financial management systems modernization.[d] Additionally, DHS issued its *Financial Systems Modernization Playbook*, which contains its plan for strengthening financial system modernization and business intelligence capabilities. DHS has created planning and guidance documents to help plan and guide components' financial system modernization projects. However, it has not yet fully developed certain guidance recommended by industry best practices that calls for developing a well documented target state of its financial management segment and a related transition plan to help effectively implement its financial system modernization approach. Additionally, components' financial systems modernization efforts are in the early planning stages. While a few DHS components have developed key planning documents, such as an analysis of alternatives and a project-specific integrated master schedule, most components have not completed other key planning documents, such as staffing plans, project plans, and concepts of operations. Further, DHS components need to develop performance and functionality targets for assessing their proposed financial systems.
Outcome No. 8: *Contractor Oversight* - Establish contractor oversight mechanisms to monitor the contractor(s) selected to implement new or upgrade existing component financial systems throughout the department.	DHS has initiated efforts to address this outcome by requiring components to establish appropriate oversight mechanisms as they proceed with their financial systems modernization, which consists of implementing new or upgrading existing component financial systems. However, as previously mentioned, components are in the early planning stages of implementing DHS's financial system modernization approach. Components have not implemented contractor oversight mechanisms because they have not hired contractors to assist with their financial systems modernization. Therefore, it is too early to determine whether components will establish effective contractor oversight mechanisms to monitor the contractor(s) selected to modernize components' financial systems. Additionally, DHS lacks an effective performance measure to monitor progress toward this outcome.
Outcome No. 9: *Financial Systems Modernization Deployment* - Successfully implement new or upgrade existing component financial systems, as needed, throughout the department, including Immigration and Customs Enforcement (ICE), USCG, and FEMA.	DHS has initiated efforts to address this outcome by having its components begin their financial systems modernization efforts.[e] However, as previously stated, these efforts are in the early planning stages, and DHS has acknowledged that many of the activities necessary to successfully implement the financial systems have not yet begun. To fully address this outcome, DHS needs to successfully deploy modernized financial systems at ICE, USCG, and FEMA.

Source: GAO analysis of DHS's June 2012, September 2012, and June 2013 *Integrated Strategy for High Risk Management* updates.

Notes: The DHS-defined assessment categories and criteria are as follows: fully addressed - outcome is fully addressed; mostly addressed - progress is significant and a small amount of work remains; partially addressed - progress is measurable, but significant work remains; and initiated - activities have been initiated to address outcome, but it is too early to report progress.

[a]In May 2012, GAO and DHS Office of the Chief Financial Officer officials agreed to revise outcomes 3, 7, 8, and 9 because the original outcomes cited DHS's Transformation and Systems Consolidation program, which had been canceled.

[b]The committee is chaired by the DHS CFO and comprises management chiefs such as the Chief Information Officer, the Chief Procurement Officer, and component CFOs.

[c]The largest reduction in the number of material weaknesses occurred for fiscal year 2007 when the auditors reported 7 material weaknesses compared to 10 for fiscal year 2006. DHS auditors' fiscal year 2007 reduction in material weaknesses was due to a consolidation of weaknesses into fewer, broader categories for reporting purposes.

[d]The guide requires information technology projects to implement best practices, such as project planning, oversight, requirements management, and standardized processes.

[e]FEMA had postponed its modernization efforts while it addressed time-sensitive, critical stability issues with its legacy financial system. FEMA had determined that its legacy system could not sustain operations while it engaged in modernization efforts. FEMA resolved its legacy system's stability issues in May 2013 and anticipates restarting its modernization efforts.

Table 4 lists the material weaknesses reported by the Department of Homeland Security's (DHS) auditors for fiscal years 2005 through 2012.

Table 4: Auditor-Reported Material Weaknesses at DHS

Number	Material weakness related to	Fiscal year							
		2005	2006	2007[a]	2008[b]	2009	2010	2011[c]	2012
1	Financial reporting	√	√	√	√			√	√
2	Financial management and reporting					√	√		
3	Financial management and entity-level controls			√					
4	Financial management and oversight	√	√						
5	Information technology controls and system functionality					√	√	√	√
6	Financial systems general and application controls				√				
7	Financial systems security	√	√	√					
8	Property, plant, and equipment (PP&E)	√	√				√	√	√
9	PP&E and operating materials and supplies					√			
10	Capital assets and supplies			√	√				
11	Operating materials and supplies	√	√						
12	Environmental and other liabilities							√	√
13	Actuarial and other liabilities			√	√	√	√		
14	Actuarial liabilities	√	√						
15	Legal and other liabilities		√						
17	Budgetary accounting	√	√	√	√	√	√	√	√
18	Fund Balance with Treasury	√	√	√	√	√	√		
19	Intragovernmental balances	√	√						
20	Undelivered orders, accounts and grants payable, and disbursements	√							
	Total number of material weaknesses	**10**	**10**	**7**	**6**	**6**	**6**	**5**	**5**

Source: GAO analysis of DHS's annual financial audit reports and *Internal Control Playbook*.

[a]For fiscal year 2007, DHS's auditors reduced the number of reported material weaknesses from 10 to 7 by consolidating the weaknesses into fewer, broader categories for reporting purposes. Specifically, the auditors combined the following: the intragovernmental balances material weakness with the financial reporting material weakness; the PP&E material weakness with the operating materials and supplies material weakness and reported the combination as capital assets and supplies for fiscal year 2007 and 2008; and the actuarial liabilities with the legal and other liabilities and reported the combination as actuarial and other liabilities in 2007 through 2010.

[b]For fiscal year 2008, the auditors concluded that the deficiencies in entity-level controls were no longer a material weakness because of DHS's remediation efforts.

[c]For fiscal year 2011, the auditors reported that DHS had mitigated the Fund Balance with Treasury material weakness.

Appendix IV: Remaining Material Weaknesses at DHS

Table 5 provides information regarding the remaining material weaknesses at the Department of Homeland Security (DHS) and the auditors' recommendations as of September 2012.

Table 5: Fiscal Year 2012 Auditor-Reported Material Weaknesses and Related Recommendations

Material weakness related to	Description of reported material weakness	Auditors' recommendations
Financial reporting: Financial reporting consisted of key financial reporting processes and internal controls.	DHS lacked effective policies, procedures, processes, and controls surrounding its financial reporting process. For example, the U.S. Coast Guard lacked a financial reporting process that completely supported beginning and year-end closeout-related activity in its three general ledgers. The Transportation Security Administration had weak supervisory reviews over capital acquisitions. Multiple components were not fully compliant with the *U.S. Standard General Ledger.*	Recommendations included developing and implementing or improving existing policies, procedures, processes, and controls related to financial reporting; training employees on the critical aspects of key supervisory review controls; and implementing general ledger systems that are compliant with the Federal Financial Management Improvement Act of 1996.
Information technology (IT) controls and financial system functionality: IT controls consisted of both general and application controls, such as access control, configuration management, and segregation of duties. Functionality relates to a financial system's ability to ensure its accuracy, confidentiality, integrity, reliability, and efficient processing.	DHS general and application controls contained numerous deficiencies. For example, access controls had deficiencies in management of application accounts, database accounts, or both and network and remote user accounts; a configuration management deficiency included the lack of evidence to support authorized modifications to key financial systems; and there was a lack of evidence to show that segregation of duties controls existed. In many cases, financial system functionality was inhibiting DHS's ability to implement and maintain internal controls, notably controls supporting financial data processing and reporting, and contributed to other control deficiencies and compliance findings.	The auditors recommended that the DHS Office of the Chief Information Officer, in coordination with the Office of the Chief Financial Officer, continue DHS's financial systems modernization initiative (which includes replacing financial systems at multiple components) and make necessary improvements to the department's financial management systems and supporting IT security controls.
Property, plant, and equipment (PP&E): PP&E consisted of personal property (i.e., aircraft, vehicles, and software), real property (i.e., land and buildings), and construction-in-process as well as stewardship and heritage assets (i.e., artwork and lighthouses).	Deficiencies within the PP&E reporting process included the lack of (1) accurate and auditable balances for personal property and construction-in-process; (2) fully designed and implemented policies, procedures, and controls to support stewardship data; and (3) adherence to procedures and processes to properly account for asset purchases and depreciation in a timely manner.	Auditors' recommended that DHS (1) continue to implement remediation efforts associated with establishing PP&E balances; (2) develop and implement policies, procedures, and controls to support supplementary information for stewardship PP&E; and (3) ensure that existing policies and procedures are followed and properly communicated.

Material weakness related to	Description of reported material weakness	Auditors' recommendations
Environmental and other liabilities: Environmental liabilities consisted of environmental remediation, cleanup, and decommissioning costs, while other liabilities were accounts payable.	Auditors noted that DHS did not ensure the completeness or accuracy of underlying data used in the calculation of environmental liability balances. Additionally, auditors stated that DHS should consider the potentially relevant current-year data on the accounts payable estimate.	Recommendations to DHS included that it (1) ensure that the existing policies and procedures over the completeness and accuracy of underlying data used in the calculation of environmental liability balances are properly followed and performed and (2) improve the enforcement of existing policies and procedures related to the accounts payable estimate.
Budgetary accounting: Budgetary accounts consist of general ledger accounts used to record transactions related to the receipt, obligation, and disbursement of appropriations.	DHS did not fully implement policies, procedures, and internal controls over budgetary processes and transactions. For example, DHS did not effectively (1) verify, validate, and monitor undelivered orders and (2) complete management reviews.	Auditors recommended that DHS develop and implement or improve and enforce existing policies and procedures related to processing, validation, and periodic reviews of budgetary transactions.

Source: GAO analysis of DHS's fiscal year 2012 annual financial audit report.

Appendix V: Comments from the Department of Homeland Security

Homeland
Security

August 27, 2013

Asif A. Khan
Director, Financial Management and Assurance
U.S. Government Accountability Office
441 G Street, NW
Washington, DC 20548

Re: Draft Report GAO-13-561, "DHS FINANCIAL MANAGEMENT: Additional Efforts
        Needed to Resolve Deficiencies in Internal Controls and Financial Management
        Systems"

Dear Mr. Khan:

Thank you for the opportunity to review and comment on this draft report. The U.S. Department
of Homeland Security (DHS) appreciates the U.S. Government Accountability Office's (GAO's)
work in planning and conducting its review and issuing this report.

As the draft report acknowledges, DHS has made considerable progress toward obtaining an
unqualified opinion on all five of its financial statements. During Fiscal Year (FY) 2012, DHS
received its first qualified audit opinion on these statements and, for the first time in its history,
provided qualified assurance on the effectiveness of internal control over financial reporting (the
first major milestone toward obtaining an opinion on internal control). These achievements
highlight the success of management integration efforts at DHS and represent important steps
toward increasing transparency and accountability for the taxpayer resources entrusted to the
Department.

DHS remains committed to further strengthening its financial management practices to better
safeguard taxpayer dollars. The Department will continue implementing its risk-based approach
to audit remediation and working closely with others to mitigate the risk of any new material
weaknesses or audit qualifications as a means to sustain continuing success. DHS is committed
to achieving an unqualified opinion on all its FY 2013 financial statements and an unqualified
opinion on its internal control over financial reporting in FY 2016.

DHS is concerned, however, that GAO's draft report appears to credit the FY 2012 audit success
to "herculean efforts, including complex workarounds that compensated for a lack of effective
controls." Although extraordinary efforts made the full-scope audit possible in FY 2012, these
efforts were primarily focused on Budgetary Accounting at the U.S. Coast Guard (USCG), where
complex workarounds were required to compensate for a lack of automated systems controls. It
is important to note that DHS is the only federal agency required to obtain an independent audit
opinion on its internal control. Components across the Department have continued to improve
internal control deficiencies through corrective actions and best practices. For example, DHS
has updated the projection in its multi-year plan to reflect Budgetary Resource Management as a

remediated material weakness in FY 2013. The Department also continues to work issues with Property, Plant, and Equipment (PPE) Accounting. Although the PPE balances will be audited in FY 2013, the material weakness will remain until FY 2014 because of the complex nature of USCG property and the disparate geographical location of assets.

The draft report also stated that DHS's independent auditors may have found additional material weaknesses had they been able to perform sufficient work to enable them to express an opinion on the effectiveness of the Department's internal control over financial reporting, which while factual, is misleading as presented. Specifically, this language is standard for a disclaimer of opinion and does not indicate that the auditors had specific significant concerns regarding any unidentified material weaknesses. Further, the auditors made this statement in conjunction with their FY 2012 scope limitation explanation, which only affected certain components of general property, plant, and equipment, and heritage and stewardship assets at USCG.

In addition, the draft report also seems to indicate that DHS's progress in remediating material weaknesses was primarily due to a refinement or consolidation of material weaknesses by the independent auditors in 2007, without providing a fuller context for this action. Since 2005, DHS has reduced by half material weaknesses in internal controls over financial reporting. The independent auditors narrowed the scope and refined the titles of several material weaknesses due to significant DHS progress achieved in remediating concerns in these areas, as well as to improve the overall presentation of the audit report's internal control exhibit.

The Department has also taken significant steps to establish and implement its Financial Systems Modernization (FSM) approach, which, as the draft report noted, is consistent with Office of Management and Budget (OMB) requirements, but otherwise seems to have not been fully reflected in the report. DHS is pursuing a decentralized approach. As each Component determines its path forward, supported by strong oversight and governance of the FSM Executive Steering Committee (ESC), it will analyze solutions with varying degrees of integration to link its financial system to asset management and acquisition systems. To complement this effort, DHS is continuing to develop a business intelligence solution to collect and aggregate data from Component systems to report Department-wide financial information and to ensure that DHS senior leadership and other key stakeholders, including Congress, have current, accurate financial information to support decision-making processes and oversight of the Homeland Security missions.

The draft report contained four recommendations, all of which the Department concurs with. Specifically, GAO recommended the Secretary of Homeland Security direct the Under Secretary for Management to:

Recommendation 1: Develop a detailed target state that describes both in technical and non-technical terms how its various Components' financial management systems will interact with each other and how information will flow among those systems.

Response: Concur. DHS agrees that a target state is essential and, as such, we have already developed and published one for the Department's modernization efforts in the DHS FSM Approach, the Chief Financial Officer (CFO) Horizon Concept of Operations, and the FSM Playbook.

2

As stated and diagramed in the aforementioned publications, DHS has adopted a decentralized strategy and will modernize individual Component financial systems, as needed. This incremental approach is consistent with OMB guidance. To support this effort, the FSM ESC will provide oversight and guidance to ensure Component modernization projects align with Department objectives and best practices. In addition, DHS will use an enterprise-level business intelligence tool to aggregate key Department-wide financial data from Component systems. Components are required to conform to Department-wide standards established by the DHS CFO, to ensure consistent enterprise-level information and reporting to internal and external stakeholders.

As each Component determines its path forward, the DHS target state will be updated accordingly. Under the target state, and as discussed with GAO during its field work for this audit, the future financial management systems will not interact nor exchange information with one another. Instead, DHS will use business intelligence tools that will collect information from each financial management system and aggregate the data into Department-wide reporting views. We request that this recommendation be considered resolved and closed.

Recommendation 2: Develop and implement a transition plan for moving from DHS's current financial management environment to the future financial management environment.

Response: Concur. DHS already has a transition strategy for moving from the Department's current financial management environment to the future financial management environment as shown in its FSM Approach document. Each Component will develop and implement a specific individual transition plan for moving from its current financial management environment to the future financial management environment on the basis of its finalized path forward. The Office of Health Affairs, for example, recently developed its transition plan to an internal shared service provider. Additionally, several other Components received the U.S. Department of the Treasury's approval to enter into the Discovery phase with a shared service provider. The Discovery phase will compare business requirements and current capabilities, facilitate the development of a project schedule, and give those Components a strong basis from which to develop a transition plan. It is important to note that timely and effective implementation of each Component's transition plan may be constrained by available funding and the federal shared service capacity to migrate additional customers. DHS will continue to collaborate with Treasury and OMB to execute our aligned strategy and will update relevant supporting documentation as each Component completes its Alternatives Analysis and finalizes its path forward. We request that this recommendation be considered resolved and closed.

Recommendation 3: Update the Standard Operating Procedures (SOP) related to the Department-level integrated master schedule (IMS) to include specific procedures for Components to revise milestone dates and provide the Office of the Chief Financial Officer (OCFO) written confirmation of completed activities to maintain accurate and timely information within the master schedule.

Response: Concur. On August 8, 2013, DHS revised its FSM Schedule Management SOP to require monthly updates to the Component IMS and posting of the updated schedule to the FSM Component SharePoint site. As a result, the DHS FSM IMS will also be updated monthly to reflect Component progress. We request that this recommendation be considered resolved and closed.

3

Recommendation 4: Include in the SOP for financial management system modernization specific procedures for consistently and systematically performing key elements of a lessons learned process including identifying lessons learned using both internal and external sources, and documenting and sharing relevant lessons learned.

Response: Concur. On August 8, 2013, DHS updated its Lessons Learned SOP to incorporate procedures for performing outreach to internal and external stakeholder to gather FSM data, including lessons learned, and to facilitate lessons learned sessions at the Financial Management Systems Working Group (FMSWG) with presentations by internal and external stakeholders.

The SOP had already prescribed how lessons learned are to be identified, documented, and shared. Specifically, Section 1.3 of the SOP states "OCFO is requiring the documentation of lessons learned as an exit criterion for each SELC [Systems Engineering Life Cycle] gate." Each Component will provide a lessons learned document prior to receiving approval at each of the eight SELC gates. Further, in the roles and responsibilities table on page 4 of the SOP, each key stakeholder group is required to enter lessons learned into a SharePoint data repository, and the Modernization Manager (MM) and the FMS Branch (FMSB) will review all items and ensure they are entered correctly.

The Department's Lessons Learned Tracking database contains a lessons learned form with required fields to ensure information is fully documented regarding the item considered to be of greatest help to other Components. The SOP requires all groups to use this database.

The SOP also states on page 4 that the MM and the FMSB will:

- Include lessons learned reviews in the monthly FMSWG and FSM ESC meetings.
- Distribute lessons learned reports to FMSWG and FSM ESC members regularly.

The specific content/subject of many DHS lessons learned is incorporated into the FSM Standards document and the DHS FSM Playbook. For example, as part of embracing best practices and as a result of associated DHS lessons learned, guidance/models on standard accounting data elements, systems testing, documenting requirements, and performing gap analysis are all included in the FSM Standards document. We request that this recommendation be considered resolved and closed.

Again, thank you for the opportunity to review and provide comment on this draft report. Technical comments were previously provided under separate cover. Please feel free to contact me if you have any questions. We look forward to working with you in the future.

Sincerely,

Jim H. Crumpacker
Director
Departmental GAO-OIG Liaison Office

4

Appendix VI: GAO Contact and Staff Acknowledgments

GAO Contact	Asif A. Khan, (202) 512-9869 or khana@gao.gov
Staff Acknowledgments	In addition to the contact named above, Michael S. LaForge (Assistant Director), Roshni C. Agarwal, LaTasha L. Freeman, Patrick T. Frey, Michael P. Holland, Jason S. Kirwan, Anh Q. Le, and Leonardo E. Zapata made key contributions to this report.

GAO's Mission	The Government Accountability Office, the audit, evaluation, and investigative arm of Congress, exists to support Congress in meeting its constitutional responsibilities and to help improve the performance and accountability of the federal government for the American people. GAO examines the use of public funds; evaluates federal programs and policies; and provides analyses, recommendations, and other assistance to help Congress make informed oversight, policy, and funding decisions. GAO's commitment to good government is reflected in its core values of accountability, integrity, and reliability.
Obtaining Copies of GAO Reports and Testimony	The fastest and easiest way to obtain copies of GAO documents at no cost is through GAO's website (http://www.gao.gov). Each weekday afternoon, GAO posts on its website newly released reports, testimony, and correspondence. To have GAO e-mail you a list of newly posted products, go to http://www.gao.gov and select "E-mail Updates."
Order by Phone	The price of each GAO publication reflects GAO's actual cost of production and distribution and depends on the number of pages in the publication and whether the publication is printed in color or black and white. Pricing and ordering information is posted on GAO's website, http://www.gao.gov/ordering.htm. Place orders by calling (202) 512-6000, toll free (866) 801-7077, or TDD (202) 512-2537. Orders may be paid for using American Express, Discover Card, MasterCard, Visa, check, or money order. Call for additional information.
Connect with GAO	Connect with GAO on Facebook, Flickr, Twitter, and YouTube. Subscribe to our RSS Feeds or E-mail Updates. Listen to our Podcasts. Visit GAO on the web at www.gao.gov.
To Report Fraud, Waste, and Abuse in Federal Programs	Contact: Website: http://www.gao.gov/fraudnet/fraudnet.htm E-mail: fraudnet@gao.gov Automated answering system: (800) 424-5454 or (202) 512-7470
Congressional Relations	Katherine Siggerud, Managing Director, siggerudk@gao.gov, (202) 512-4400, U.S. Government Accountability Office, 441 G Street NW, Room 7125, Washington, DC 20548
Public Affairs	Chuck Young, Managing Director, youngc1@gao.gov, (202) 512-4800 U.S. Government Accountability Office, 441 G Street NW, Room 7149 Washington, DC 20548